Attitude Adjustments

Skits For Retreats And Worship

Linda R. Tippett

CSS Publishing Company, Inc., Lima, Ohio

ATTITUDE ADJUSTMENTS

ISBN: 0-7880-0765-3

*To my husband for his continuing love and patience
... and to the members of Pilgrim Church, United
Church of Christ in Toledo, Ohio, for their support
and encouragement through the years.*

Table Of Contents

Preface

The subjects covered in this collection — greed, pride, guilt, forgiveness — are all such an integral part of our human condition that I wanted to investigate each one with a down-to-earth approach that would appeal to everyone. Perhaps you can see yourself in one or all of the playlets, and then find some inspiration in the short meditations that follow each one. I hope the prayers will touch a chord that resonates in your life and put into words what you may have been struggling with for a week or a year. And then I hope you will want to share these short services with others as you find the need to present something meaningful to a group. They're easy to do and they're God-inspired. May they bring peace to all who hear.

Shalom

Linda R. Tippett

I Can't Forgive The Whole World

Length: Approximately four or five minutes

Characters
Harold — middle-aged, middle-class harried businessman
Edna — his well-meaning but flighty wife
Gary — their unpredictable teenage son
Ed — their neighbor who has borrowed once too often

Scene
Audience will be told to imagine Harold and Edna's family room. The only furniture needed is a stand with a phone on it. As the curtain opens, Harold is on the phone.

Harold: *(Quite agitated)* Now listen here, Sheldon. I gave you five thousand dollars to invest in those stocks that you *swore* couldn't lose ... now you're telling me what? *(He listens and gets more agitated)* I don't care if the Dow-Jones jumped in the *lake!* You said my five thousand would be safe and I trusted you! What kind of a stockbroker are you, anyway? *(Listens)* That's right, a lousy one! I don't care if you *do* have family problems, that doesn't get my money back. So what are you gonna do about it?

(Edna enters, wringing her hands and looking flustered)

Edna: Oh, Harold, quick. I've got to tell you something!

Harold: *(To Edna, annoyed)* Can't you see I'm on the phone? Wait for me in the kitchen!

9

Edna: But I've gotta tell you ...

(Harold points off stage, and says "Go!" She goes)

Harold: *(To phone)* No ... not you, Sheldon! Listen, I want you to tell me just what I'm supposed to do now? *(Listens ... and grows incredulous) Forgive* you? You're kidding! I'm out five thousand bucks and I'm supposed to forgive you ... just because your wife's sick and your kid's in jail?

(Edna enters again ... looking even more flustered, still wringing her hands)

Edna: Harold, I've just got to tell you ...

Harold: *(To Edna in exasperation ... and pointing offstage)* Back to the kitchen! *(She starts to go then stops and listens) (Harold to phone)* No, not you, Sheldon. Listen, buddy, I'm gonna hang up now, but when I call you tomorrow, you'd better have my five thousand bucks, you understand? *(Slams down the phone)* Forgive him? He's out of his mind!

Edna: *(Starts in again and then it sinks in)* Harold, I've just got to tell you ... wait a minute ... *(Gasps)* you lost five thousand dollars?

Harold: Forget it, Edna, forget it! *(Tightlipped)* Now, what do you want?

Edna: *(Now rather scared and breathless)* Well ... you'd better come out to the garage ... because I put the car in the wrong gear and now the garage is sort of open at both ends.

Harold: *(Incredulous)* You what? You idiot! I don't believe this. You're stupid, Edna, stupid!

Edna: *(Wailing)* I didn't do it on purpose, Harold, honest I didn't! Please forgive me!

Harold: *(Angrily)* Forgive you? Do you know how much this is going to cost? You and your dumb accidents! This is really the last straw, Edna.

Edna: *(Still wailing)* Oh, Harold, I'm sorry.

(At this point, Gary enters as if in a big hurry)

Gary: Hey, what happened to the garage?

Harold: *(Disgusted)* Your mother's been redecorating again. Don't ask!

Gary: *(Looking from one to the other)* Oh! *(Pauses)* Well, hey, Dad, I've really got to talk to you.

Harold: *(Sighs)* So what else is new? Join the group!

Gary: *(Confused)* What?

Harold: *(Resigned)* Never mind. What's with you?

Gary: *(Hesitant, then says it quickly all at once, looking first at one and then the other)* Well-l-l, I need some money because Debbie and I want to get married and we ...

Edna: *(Puts her hand over her mouth)* Oh, no!

Harold: *(Aghast)* Stop right there! What do you mean you want to get married? You're still in high school!

Gary: *(Very nervous)* I know that ... but we really want to ... because Debbie's pregnant ... and ...

11

Edna: *(Wailing)* Oh, *no*!

Harold: I knew it. I knew it would happen! Didn't I tell you, Edna? That girl was after Gary, and she'd get him any way she could.

Gary: *(Protesting)* No, no, Dad! We're really in love, and we didn't mean for this to happen. You've got to forgive us ...

Harold: *(Quite agitated)* Forgive you! You've just ruined your life and you expect me to say it's okay? You're crazy!

*(Suddenly there's a knock at the door and Ed, the neighbor, enters. The group is **not** pleased to see him)*

Ed: *(Brightly and oblivious to the situation)* Hey, hi, guys! How's it goin'? Boy, I'm glad you're home, Harold, old buddy. I've got to talk to you. *(Stops and looks from one to the other)* Oh, hey, did I come at a bad time? *(But plows on)* Yeah, but this won't take a second. Harold, old buddy, you know the power mower you let me borrow? Well, I kind of had an accident ... and you've got to forgive me, buddy ... but I ...

(Harold claps both hands on his head, then throws his arms up in the air)

Harold: *(In anguish)* Dear God, I can't forgive the whole world!

End

Order Of Worship

Call To Worship
L: Lift up your hearts!
C: We lift them, Lord, to thee;
Here at thy feet none other may we see.
L: Lift up your hearts!
C: Even so, with one accord,
We lift them up, we lift them to the Lord.
— From hymn "Lift Up Your Hearts!"
Henry M. Butler
Walter Greatorex

Prayer
Oh, dear God, you have taught us through Jesus to be sensitive to
others' needs, to always find the good in our neighbors. Now we
ask that you give us the grace and power within ourselves to follow your teachings ... not only to find the needs and the good, but
in getting there to have the strength to forgive the roadblocks that
may be thrown up against us. Help us to remember that when we
forgive we reverse the flow of pain that began with a real or imag-
ined hurt ... a flow that wounds our present and poisons our future.
We heal ourselves. It can be like a miracle, for we create a new
beginning and again walk hand in hand with you. Help us to know
that in forgiving we find a new freedom, a freedom to throw open
wide our souls to receive you fully, and live a life that carries no
past unpleasant baggage. We thank you, in Jesus' name. Amen.

Responsive Reading Or Litany
L: Keep your promise, Lord, and forgive my sins.
C: For they are many.
L: Those who obey the Lord

C: **Will learn from him the path they should follow.**
L: They will always be prosperous,
C: **And their children will possess the land.**
L: The Lord is the friend of those who obey him
C: **And He affirms his covenant with them.**
L: I look to the Lord for help at all times,
C: **And He rescues me from danger.**
L: Turn to me, Lord, and be merciful to me,
C: **Because I am lonely and weak.**
L: Relieve me of my worries
C: **And save me from all my troubles.**
L: Consider my distress and suffering
C: **And forgive all my sins.**

— Psalm 25:11-18

Scripture Readings
Luke 7:36-50
Colossians 3:12-13

Play: *"I Can't Forgive The Whole World"*

Meditation

The Lord's Prayer

Benediction
May God bless and keep you. May the forgiving Lord make his face to shine upon you and be gracious unto you; in your going out and in your coming in, in your lying down and in your rising up, in your labor and in your leisure, in your laughter and in your tears, until at last you stand in his presence, world without end. Amen.

Meditation

He can't forgive the whole world? Why not? Jesus did.

Some of the very last words Jesus said were "Forgive them, Father, for they know not what they do." But that was just the culmination of the many acts of forgiveness that Jesus performed and talked about during his ministry on earth. Forgiveness was a cornerstone of his teachings. Even the prayer he taught us says, "… and forgive our debts as we forgive our debtors." (Or "trespasses.") We're asked to pray to God to forgive our sins as we have supposedly forgiven those who have sinned against us. Forgive — even love — our enemies? Turn the other cheek? Yes. These are some of God's instructions given through Jesus, and if we are to be practicing Christians, we need to pay attention.

You may have noticed I said that in the prayer we ask to be forgiven our sins as we have *supposedly* forgiven those who have sinned against us. Well, God assumes that we have followed his instructions. He is kind of like our grandparents. He thinks we are always good and if we're bad and are sorry, he forgives us. He wants us to be like him.

But in reality you and I know how hard it is to forgive someone who has really hurt us, or disappointed and exasperated us. We know what we're *supposed* to do; God through Jesus has made that clear. But he also made us human, with all the feelings and emotions and relationships that can get as tangled as coat hangers in a closet. We find ourselves hurting and hating till we lose sight of healing and the happiness that can come with forgiveness.

In the play, Harold is asked to forgive four times: an associate who made a wrong decision that cost Harold his hard-earned money; a wife whose continuing small disasters seem to reach a climax; a son who is in trouble; and a neighbor who accidentally destroyed a borrowed possession. It makes little difference that none of the

15

hurts was intentional. He perceives them as such and in his exasperation he fails to see how any forgiveness can take place. But it can.

What is forgiving? In his book *Forgive and Forget*, Lewis B. Smedes says, "The act of forgiving, by itself, is a wonderfully simple act — but it always happens inside a storm of complex emotions. It is the hardest trick in the whole bag of personal relationships. We forgive in four stages: *Hurt* — when somebody causes you pain so deep and unfair you cannot forget it; *Hate* — you cannot shake the memory of how much you were hurt, and you cannot wish your enemy well. You sometimes want the person who hurt you to suffer as you are suffering; *Healing* — you are given the insight to see the person who hurt you in a new light. Your memory is healed, the pain recedes and you are free again; *The Coming Together* — you invite the person who hurt you back into your life."

One of the key phrases in Mr. Smedes' discussion is "you are free again." Many times we don't realize that as long as we hold a grudge against someone, that person still has a power over us that can sit like a stone in our soul. We need to break that power by following God's instructions, praying that he help us set aside the hurt and hate, and get on with the healing and coming together.

There's a Harold in all of us, but we don't need to forgive the whole world. Just one person at a time. Amen.

Guilty As Charged

Length: Approximately three minutes

Characters
Pat Johnson — a long-suffering wife and mother
Jim Johnson — a long-suffering son, husband, and father
Jodi Johnson — their long-suffering teenage daughter

Scene
The Johnsons' living room. Three chairs are needed. Pat is sitting
on one doing needlework and Jim is on one reading the paper. A
small stand with a telephone is by Jim's chair.

Pat: So, you didn't answer me. When was the last time you called
your mother?

Jim: *(From behind the paper)* I don't know.

Pat: *(Emphatically)* Well, *I* know. It's been at least a month, I'll
bet, and you know she won't call us because, as she keeps saying,
it costs money to call long distance. And as she also keeps saying,
she only has her social security. We have so much more, and it
wouldn't hurt us just to call her once in a while, and let her know
we're still alive. You know she always says hearing from you is
one of the few pleasures she has left in this world.

Jim: *(Looking over the top of the paper)* Come on, Pat. I know
what she says. That's why I don't call her.

Pat: *(Slightly self-righteous)* Well, it seems to me that you could listen to it for a few minutes maybe every other week. She *is* lonesome and she doesn't get out. It just wouldn't hurt you to make the effort. It's not like she has other children, you know. You *are* the only one.

Jim: How well I know! She reminds me every chance she gets! Listen, she has guilt trips she hasn't even used, and I don't need one from you right now. *(Goes behind the paper again)* I'll call her when I'm good and ready.

Pat: *(Insistent)* Call her now, Jim. You just never know how long she's going to be around. Now if she were my mother ...

Jim: *(Throws the paper down in exasperation)* Take her ... she's yours! *(Pauses)* ALL RIGHT! I'll call her!

Pat: When?

Jim: *(Still exasperated)* Oh, for Pete's sake! Tonight. I'll call her tonight!

Pat: You say it, but you won't do it.

Jim: *(Getting angry)* Listen, if you don't knock this off ...

(At this moment Jodi comes in from outside, takes her coat off, throws it on the empty chair, and starts to pick up the phone without saying anything to her parents)

Jim: *(Still angry)* Wait a minute, young lady! Not so fast. I'm just about to call your grandmother! *(Pauses and then really lets his anger out)* And, incidentally, just where have you been? Your mother's been waiting here for you to help her with supper, and God knows what else, and you've been out running around with your friends, probably at the stupid mall, having a good time, never thinking of your family and the help they need, always thinking of

18

yourself. And maybe I needed the car. You ever think of that? Oh, no. Or would you ever call to find out? And what did you ...

Jodi: *(Interrupting and a bit angry, too) You* wait a minute, Daddy! You said I could have the car all afternoon, remember? And it's not even dinnertime yet. And Mom didn't say anything about needing help, so what's the problem?

Pat: *(Smugly)* The problem is he doesn't want to call your grandmother!

(Jim disappears behind his paper)

Jodi: *(Angrily)* Well, he doesn't need to take it out on me! *(Goes to the phone)* I've really got to make this call. *(Dials the phone then slams it down in disgust)* Busy! I'll bet he's talking to that sneaky Jennifer. She'd just better keep her hands off my boyfriend! *(Turns to her mother)* Mom, did you take in those jeans like I asked you to?

Pat: *(Guiltily)* Oh no, I completely forgot. I'm sorry. When do you need them?

Jodi: *(Sarcastically)* Well, I wanted them for tonight to go out with Todd. I asked you this morning and you've just been sitting around doing your dumb needlework *(Now angrily and near tears)* and now I won't have anything to wear and I'll lose Todd to that stupid Jennifer and it's all your fault! *(She runs from the room)*

Pat: *(Sighs and goes back to her needlework)* Well, guilty as charged again, I guess.

(Jim now lowers his paper and starts dialing the phone)

Jim: Hello, Mom? *(Listens, then shouts)* WHAT DO YOU MEAN, WHO IS THIS?

End

Order Of Worship

Call To Worship
L: God is here — let's celebrate!
C: He is just — and He is forgiving.
L: He gently picks up those who have fallen.
C: He sustains those who are wavering in weakness.
L: He is near enough to hear our every cry.
C: God is here — let's celebrate!

Prayer
Dear Lord, we do celebrate you. We celebrate your nearness and we know you will not cop out on your promises to us. We know you will grant us whatever is necessary to make us happy and productive and fill our hungry hearts. We know all this, and yet we wonder why so much of the time we walk around full of guilt for things done or undone. Why on some days do we feel that we've screwed up completely and things will never be right and the guilt hangs like a stone around our necks? We know you made us human with the power to make life difficult for ourselves, but, Lord, we need to know that you're there to keep us strong, to fight our feelings of inadequacy. We don't need to feel responsible for everything that goes wrong around us, do we, Lord? You have the power to enter our hearts and minds to quiet our uneasy fears and distorted judgments. We ask that you bring us once again your grace and healing and soothe our foolish ways. We need to be reminded that you never leave us, even when we forget to look for you. Please breathe your Holy Spirit into our lives once again. We pray in Jesus' name. Amen.

Responsive Reading Or Litany

L: Praise the Lord, O my soul,

C: Do not forget how kind He is.

L: He is slow to become angry,

C: And is full of constant love.

L: He does not punish us as we deserve,

C: Or repay us for our sins and wrongs.

L: He so blesses us with love and mercy,

C: That we need not fear our insecurities and guilts.

L: As high as the sky is above the earth,

C: So great is his love for those who have reverence for him.

L: As kind as a father is to his children,

C: So kind is the Lord to those who honor him.

Scripture Reading
Isaiah 6:1-7

Play: *"Guilty As Charged"*

Meditation

Benediction
May God bless and keep you. May the Lord who understands our frailties and weaknesses make his face to shine upon you and be gracious unto you; in your going out and in your coming in, in your lying down and in your rising up, in your labor and in your leisure, in your laughter and in your tears, until at last you stand in his presence, world without end. Amen.

Meditation

Does Pat's last statement, "Guilty as charged, again," sound familiar in our lives? Of course it does, because sooner or later we all feel like Pat — guilty. It's one of the absolutes in our lives. As Paula and Dick McDonald put it in their book *Guilt Free,* "Most of us walk around much of the time feeling guilty about something; guilty of not living up to our own or to other people's standards; guilty because we don't measure up — at least not consistently — to society's image of the 'good mother,' the 'good father,' the 'good son or daughter,' the 'good citizen,' the 'good provider'; guilty because what we once learned as right and nice and good no longer seems to apply; guilty because we're in a world of conflicting expectations and can't seem to please everyone."

Let's look at the family we just visited. Guilt hangs in the air like a thundercloud. We see it passing through the family in several different forms. From mother to son, from wife to husband, from father to daughter, from daughter to mother. Jim's angry outburst at Jodi is a direct result of the guilt trip laid on him by his wife. Jodi lashes out at her mother because of her insecurity with her boyfriend. And in the end Jim unleashes his exasperation back at his mother. So we can see that in close relationships guilt can erupt into a vicious cycle.

It can even in one sense be called "our number one killer." Psychologists say that it far surpasses cancer and heart failure, accidents, addictions, suicides, and murders, for guilt is a major contributor to all these. Guilt may drive us to suffer physical illness, to commit an accident, to become an addict, to be driven to suicide or murder. Guilt is almost always at the bottom of deep depression. If we could get rid of much of the irrational guilt we carry around, many of us would live longer without unnecessary pain.

And it doesn't have to be major guilt, like what Judas eventually felt, for example. It can be just feeling guilty when it isn't necessary — the common small guilts we each experience daily that hang us up, wear us down, and waste our energy.

You feel guilty because you're having a crabby day, because you don't want to do one more blasted flash card with your child, because you hid the last four Oreos to eat by yourself, because you forgot a friend's birthday, because you forgot to call your mother, because you'd rather watch television than clean the house or garage or whatever, because today you can't stand your two-year-old, because you resent your sister or brother because they're better looking and have more money, because you yelled at your kids when you fought with your boss, because ... because ... because ... it goes on and on.

These seemingly insignificant events can accumulate over time and stop us from reaching the fullness of life that God intended for us. We have so many "shoulds" and "should not's" echoing from our childhood and expectations from the current world around us — family, friends, work — that we think we just can't live up to them all. Some days we just throw in the towel.

Mothers are a good example, especially in these days of career tracks and day care. Paula McDonald says, "Mothers haven't a prayer of navigating this life guilt-free. No group in history has been as consistently idealized, or given higher or more difficult expectations to live up to. It's easier to be a good Marine than a good mother. If your child grows up to be Marvin Marvel, take a bow. If he doesn't, it's all your fault."

Lots of free guilt trips there! But this is an ideal place to remember that all of us do some of it well, and some of us do all of it well some of the time, but none of us does all of it well all of the time. It isn't possible. That includes being a mother or just getting through life in general.

So we need to shake off these guilts. And how do we do this? Well, certainly God did not intend for us to walk around so constantly burdened. Remember, he sent Jesus to tell us that we should love our neighbor as ourselves. Now there are two messages there, but the important one for us in this discussion is the second one. To love ourselves is to be strong enough to believe that we are, indeed, the best persons we can be and we can let no one lay a guilt trip on us unless we choose to accept it. Remember Jodi's response to her father's angry tirade? She knew she wasn't guilty and she let him know it. She had the healthiest self-esteem in that family.

As Norman Vincent Peale says, "It is of practical value to learn to like yourself. Since you must spend so much time with yourself, you might as well get some satisfaction out of the relationship."

So God intends for us to be whole and healthy, to accept the blessings of self-acceptance, inner peace, and love for others. His help is there for the asking ... with no guilt trips attached. Amen.

Greed Is Where You Find It

Length: Approximately three-and-a-half minutes

Characters
Betty — a sentimental daughter
Carol — a less than sentimental daughter
Arnold — a son with a weakness

Scene
An attic in a big, old home. Props needed are an old trunk (or very large cardboard box), two chairs, four or five medium-size boxes, a large book, an old photo album, a coat tree, several ugly dresses and an old fur coat. Boxes, book, and album are in the trunk. The dresses and coat are hanging on the coat tree. As the scene opens, Betty is holding one of the dresses up in front of her and Arnold is seated by the trunk looking through the boxes.

Betty: What do you think, Arnold? I always thought Mom had good taste and she bought expensive things. I'll bet this will come back in style.

Arnold: *(Engrossed in looking in the trunk)* Huh? What'd you say?

Betty: *(Exasperated)* Will you please get your nose out of that trunk and tell me what you think about these clothes? I want to grab them before Carol gets here, if you think they're worthwhile.

Arnold: *(Looking up)* Yeah, sure. They're fine. *(Sniffs)* If you don't mind that stinky old perfume! Mom sure liked to pour it on! *(Betty* *sniffs the dress, makes a face and quickly hangs the dress back on the coat tree. Then she sits down on the other chair and starts looking through the trunk with Arnold, who is finding interesting things)* Hey, there's lots of good stuff in here. Why, here's Dad's coin collection! *(Holds up medium-size box and pauses)* You know, Mom was real sneaky. She knew I wanted this in the worst way after Dad died. So she hid it. She knew I'd never look up here. *(Angrily)* Bless her heart!

Betty: *(Shrugs)* Well, let's face it. She knew you couldn't be trusted to keep it intact. You would've sold it, right? And gambled the money away. She knew what she was doing right to the end.

Arnold: *(Petulantly)* Well, it's mine now. And I can do what I want.

Betty: *(A bit nasty)* How do you know it's yours? Mom's will said everything should be divided three ways, and we'll have to wait till Carol gets here.

Arnold: *(A short laugh)* Oh, Miss Holier-Than-Thou! Who just said she wanted the clothes before Carol saw them?

Betty: *(Tossing her head)* That's different. Carol's got too many clothes now. And these are kind of sentimental. They *were* Mom's, even if they do smell funny. And Carol doesn't have a sentimental bone in her body. All she wants is the valuable stuff, as if she needed it.

Arnold: So where is she, anyway? She's the one who wanted to get this stuff cleared out.

Betty: *(Sarcastically)* She probably can't tear herself away from her bridge game at her fancy country club. Or maybe her big expensive Cadillac wouldn't start. Wouldn't that be a hoot?

Arnold: *(Listening)* Wait a minute. I think I hear her.

(Carol breezes in hurriedly, stylishly dressed and wearing a fur coat)

Carol: *(Brightly)* Well, what's going on? Have you two got all the good stuff? I'll bet you didn't wait for me at all. Remember what the will said — split it all three ways.

Betty: *(Evenly)* No, we don't have all the good stuff. We're just looking through things. You're welcome to do the same, and then we'll decide.

Carol: *(Busily)* All right, now just let me look. *(She leans over the trunk and starts opening boxes)* Well, what do you know! Here's all that clunky antique jewelry Mom used to wear. I'll bet that's worth something. I'll just take *all* that ... *(She looks at the box Arnold's holding)* ... and Dad's coin collection! I want that, too.

Arnold: *(Protesting)* Wait a minute! Mom promised that to me!

Betty: *(Disapproving)* Arnold!

Carol: *(Emphatically)* She did no such thing! That's a lie and you know it! She didn't want it winding up in some pawnshop. So I'll just take it and you won't be tempted. *(Arnold hangs onto the box, and turns his back on her)* Don't be like that, Arnold. You know I'm right! *(She looks at Betty, who is leafing through the photograph album)* Well, *you* can have that. I certainly don't want any reminders of how geeky I looked as a kid! Old pictures are a bore! *(Reaches into the trunk and pulls out the book and leafs through it)* But this looks like a first edition. Yes, it is. So I'll take this, too. *(Gestures at the coat tree)* And you can have those old dresses. Mom had terrible taste. But I *do* want that fur coat! *(Gets it off the coat tree)*

Betty: *(A bit aghast)* But you've *got* a fur coat!

27

Carol: *(Smugly)* Well, one just never can have too many furs, don't you think? *(Starts gathering up boxes and the book, etc.)*

Arnold: *(Still hanging on tightly to his box)* I don't believe you! You've got everything in the world! So what do you want with all this stuff? You're just plain greedy!

Carol: *(She grabs the box of coins from him and with her arms full of coat, boxes, and book, starts out the door and says airily)* Well, so what! You know what they always say. You can't be too rich or too thin! Ta Ta!

End

Order Of Worship

Call To Worship
L: Behold us, Lord,
C: In a space from daily tasks set free,
L: Behold us, Lord,
C: We meet to rest a little while with thee.
L: Behold us, Lord,
C: As we shed our heavy loads of care,
L: Behold us, Lord,
C: We look up, then lift our hearts in prayer.

Prayer
Dear God, is this a day like every other day? Is this a day when routine rules our lives, dulls our vision, and blunts our judgment? Will we go charging blindly through the day carelessly hurting others, shrinking from our responsibilities, complaining about almost everything? We're asking, Lord, because we need a different direction. We don't want another humdrum day that magnifies our faults. We want to know the excitement of seeing our lives suddenly washed in brilliant colors, of knowing that we have left a trail of light behind us as the day wears on. We want to know how to reach out in love and know that someone feels our touch. But, Lord, are we being greedy to want so much so fast? We know instant gratification is a form of greed. So show us your way, Lord. Give us the patience to wait as we ask for your Holy Spirit to work its wonders in us and our lives, leaving our greedy thoughts in the dust and enriching our days. Hear us as we pray in Jesus' name. Amen.

Responsive Reading Or Litany

L: Teach me, Lord, the meaning of your laws,

C: And I will obey them at all times.

L: Explain your law to me, and I will obey it:

C: I will keep it with all my heart.

L: Keep me obedient to your commandments,

C: Because in them I find happiness.

L: Give me the desire to obey your laws

C: Rather than to get rich.

L: Keep me from paying attention to what is worthless;

C: Be good to me, as you have promised.

L: Enable me to speak the truth at all times,

C: Because my hope is in your judgments.

L: I will live in perfect freedom,

C: Because I try to obey your teachings.

— Psalm 119:33-37, 43, 45

Scripture Reading
Luke 12:15-21

Play: *"Greed Is Where You Find It"*

Meditation

Benediction
May God bless and keep you. May the Lord who helps us guard against greed make his face to shine upon you and be gracious unto you; in your going out and in your coming in, in your lying down and in your rising up, in your labor and in your leisure, in your laughter and in your tears, until at last you stand in his presence, world without end. Amen.

Meditation

You can't be too rich? Well, certainly Jesus thought so. Remember the story in the New Testament when he encountered the rich young man who asked, "What good deed must I do to have eternal life?" Jesus had little patience with him because he sensed his arrogance, so he looked him up and down and answered, "If you want to be perfect, go and sell all you have and give the money to the poor, and you will have riches in heaven. Then come and follow me."

Now that was a straight answer if there ever was one, and the rich young man didn't take it well. Maybe he thought Jesus was joking, just having a little fun because the man was obviously rich and Jesus wanted a big reaction. Maybe, because all the disciples were around them, he thought Jesus was playing to the crowd. So he got mad. Perhaps he thought this was just a dusty preacher from out of nowhere after all who had no right to make those kinds of demands on him. Was the man making fun of him? He didn't stay to find out and turned and stalked away with as much dignity as he could manage. And that's when he heard Jesus say to his disciples, in a sad sort of way, "It is much harder for a rich person to enter the Kingdom of God than for a camel to go through the eye of a needle." Do you suppose the young man ever wondered what that meant? Maybe. But we'll never know.

Now let's look at that story again and this time put Carol in the role of the rich young man. Let's suppose that at one point in her life she was greedy enough to think that she could buy her way into heaven, if not with money, then maybe with good deeds. She'd be willing to put herself out a *little* bit if she could be sure of a ticket to eternal bliss. After all, she considered herself a Christian. She heard of a preacher who specialized in good deeds and decided to catch one of his sermons. It would be easy because he

31

liked to preach outdoors. Her husband sighed at the thought of one more of her selfish obsessions, but didn't discourage her. She watched for news that the preacher would be in her area and caught up with him one day. She pushed her way to the front of the crowd, and when he was done preaching, she went right up to him and asked, "And what good deed must *I* do to get into heaven?" The preacher sized her up with one glance and said, "Sell all you have and give the money to the poor and follow Jesus' way!" She couldn't believe it! Not what she had in mind. Then the man talked about a camel and a needle, but she ignored it. The only camel she knew was her expensive camel's hair coat and she hadn't picked up a needle for years. So she stormed home and dismissed the whole idea. And, as we saw, she was still consumed with unrepentant greed.

So we can see it's no easier to part with material goods in this century than it was in Jesus' time, even after all the centuries of retelling the way Jesus would have us live. He knew greed is a basic human trait and tried to leave blueprints to guide us into acceptable compromises. Neither Carol or the rich young man understood that following Jesus' way would teach them that "selling all you have and giving the money to the poor" need not be an absolute. He was looking for an awareness that some kind of sacrifice is needed in order to live the Christian life. Tithing is a good example of what he might have had in mind. Those who tithe regularly report an extraordinary kind of peace and fulfillment in their lives. There are other ways, but when the Carol in us threatens to get out of hand we need to understand that greed must be tempered with giving. It can be an enriching experience. Amen.

Too Proud To Be Too Proud

Length: Approximately three-and-a-half minutes

Characters
Marge Williams — a social-climbing housewife with big ideas
Ellen Anderson — her disillusioned friend

Scene
Marge's kitchen. A small table and two chairs will be needed with two coffee mugs and a coffee pot on the table. The women are seated at the table. They will be drinking coffee throughout the skit.

Marge: *(Pouring the coffee)* I'm so glad you came over, Ellen. I've got all these great ideas about the programs for the Women's Club, and I want to tell you what I'm planning.

Ellen: *(Guardedly)* Wait a minute ... *you're* planning! What about the program committee?

Marge: *(Proudly)* Oh, well, *I'm* the one they elected president, you know. And I think I ought to be the one who has the say over what kind of things we hear this year. And besides, that committee is full of fuddy-duddies. They'll talk it to death.

Ellen: *(Somewhat grimly)* Be careful, Marge. My sister is on that committee, you know.

Marge: *(Airily)* Oh well, your sister's all right, I guess, but the rest of them ... *(Makes a dismissing gesture and then is distracted to a new topic)* Oh, remind me! Before you leave I want to show you my new living room. The decorator just finished, and I think it would be the perfect place to have the club's first meeting, don't you?

Ellen: *(Protesting)* But you know we always have the first meeting of the year at Edna Miller's. She was our first president and it's tradition. She looks forward to it. You *know* she's getting older.

Marge: *(A little nasty)* Well, she also has the tackiest living room in this town, and I'm tired of it. And since I'm president now I think I ought to be able to say where we meet. *(Petulantly)* Besides, what good is it to spend all that money on new things if I can't show them off?

Ellen: *(Still protesting)* But that isn't what the club bylaws say.

Marge: *(Smiling)* What ... I can't show off my new living room?

Ellen: *(Emphatically)* You know what I mean. Just because you're president you can't just go changing the rules to suit yourself.

Marge: *(Tossing her head)* Nobody follows those old bylaws anyway! And I can make up my own rules. My husband does it all the time in his business and it works for him. And he can buy and sell anyone in this town ... with money left over!

Ellen: Hey, we're not talking about Ralph and his used car business here. We're talking about the club!

Marge: *(Again rather nasty)* Well, I guess what I'm trying to say is that we're pretty important people in this town, and it wouldn't be to anyone's advantage to push her own ideas in the club this year ... if you know what I mean.

Ellen: *(Aghast and sort of chokes on her coffee)* I can't believe what I'm hearing. Is that a threat? This is just a little old women's club, Marge. If you want to be a dictator, go find yourself a country!

Marge: *(Proudly)* Well! It just may be a little old women's club to you, Ellen Anderson, but as far as I'm concerned it's THE club in town and I've worked long and hard to be president. And I'm proud of it. And I'm going to be the best one the club's ever had. So there!

Ellen: *(Grimly)* No matter who gets hurt, right?

Marge: *(Shrugging)* I'm just not going to let some old fuddy-duddies get in my way.

Ellen: *(Angrily getting up from her chair)* Well, here's one that's going to get *out* of your way ... right now! I'm leaving. You can take your fall by yourself!

Marge: What do you mean, my fall?

Ellen: *(Still angry)* You know, like in the Bible — what pride goeth before!

Marge: *(Sees that Ellen really means to go and starts to laugh)* Ellen, Ellen, come on back. I'm only kidding! I just wanted to see how far I could tease you. I didn't mean any of those things I said. Don't go! It was just a joke! *(Eagerly)* Don't you see ...?

Ellen: *(Stops halfway to the door and just looks at Marge for a few seconds, then says)* Yes, I do see. And guess what? The joke's on you, Marge. Now you're too proud to admit you're too proud! *(She moves toward the door)* Thanks for the coffee. See you around. *(Stops again)* And by the way, I saw your living room on my way in. I'd really get another decorator if I were you, Marge. Tacky, tacky!

End

35

Order Of Worship

Call To Worship
L: Lift up our hearts, O King of kings,
C: To brighter hopes and kindlier things,
L: To visions of a larger good,
C: And holier dreams of brotherhood.
L: Your world is weary of its pain,
C: Of selfish greed and fruitless gain.
L: Look down on all earth's sin and strife
C: And lift us to a nobler life.

— Hymn "Lift Up Our Hearts"
John H.B. Masterman

Prayer
Dear Lord, sometimes we feel so burdened with the world's pain
and sin and strife that all we want is just a single breath of fresh air
or to flee to some ivory tower, far away from what seems constant
insanity and inhumanity. We feel as if we're in a circle of darkness,
continually trapped without light. We know you're there, Lord, but
we need a sign. Please renew in us a vision of a world where there
is no deceitful pride or greed. Let us know once again that there is
within ourselves the power to overcome these destructive forces
that can tear our own lives and the world apart. Make us aware of
the sustaining strength of your presence — a strength that enables
us to hold steady through the dark nights of our souls. Let us know
that there is work in the world to be done, work that perhaps only
we can do. Keep us from letting our pride or laziness get in the
way of what you would have us accomplish in our lives and in the
world. Bless us with your spirit, in Jesus' name we pray. Amen.

Responsive Reading Or Litany
L: Lord, I have given up my pride,
C: **And turned away from my arrogance.**
L: So place a guard at my mouth
C: **And a sentry at the door of my lips.**
L: Keep me from wanting to do wrong
C: **And from joining evil people in their wickedness.**
L: Because your love is constant, hear me, O Lord,
C: **Show your mercy and preserve my resolve.**

Scripture Reading
Proverbs 16:18-19
Proverbs 29:23
Proverbs 11:2

Play: *"Too Proud To Be Too Proud"*

Meditation

Benediction
May God bless and keep you. May the Lord, who lets us take a fall
from pride but always picks us up, make his face to shine upon you
and be gracious unto you; in your going out and in your coming in,
in your lying down and in your rising up, in your labor and in your
leisure, in your laughter and in your tears, until at last you stand in
his presence, world without end. Amen.

Meditation

Yes, "tacky, tacky," indeed! Ellen couldn't resist that parting shot, even if it did show a little meanness of spirit. But who could blame her? Marge had definitely set herself up for it. That's one of the evils of excessive pride. It has a way of bringing out the worst in those on the receiving end — a two-edged sword, so to speak. Marge was swelling with self-importance, all primed to ride roughshod over the feelings of others while Ellen was getting more outraged by the minute and finally had the devastating last word.

What do you think Marge did after Ellen left? Did she suddenly realize what she had said, and what those words meant? Did she break down in tears, hurt by Ellen's remark? Or did she shrug her shoulders and think, "Well, if she can't take it, who needs her?" Mostly the latter, I'm afraid.

Marge was "filled with herself," with her own self-importance. Though she may have had her moments of truly wanting to be liked, she didn't mind stepping on people on the way up the power ladder. And she was probably trying to get Ellen to go along with her idea. But then when Ellen proved not to be just another rung on the ladder, Marge hastily tried to back off, sensing the making of a new enemy. And her pride wouldn't let her admit she had done the wrong thing.

Keith Miller, in his book *Sin — Overcoming the Ultimate Deadly Addiction,* quotes William Temple as saying, "There is only one Sin, and it is characteristic of the whole world. It is the self-will which prefers 'my way' to God's — which puts 'me' in the center where only God should be in place." In other words — pride!

Miller further says, "There is a frightening and tenacious quality about this deeply imbedded tendency to put ourselves in the center and try to get our own way. It seems to defy the most powerful efforts of our human will to change it." Look at the old story of Adam and Eve. They were put into a virtual paradise — owned and operated by God — and were told what they could and could not do. Still, as soon as they were left alone, they tried to be God. They were in paradise, but they wanted to be "Number One."

And we know what happened. They fouled up all their relationships — to God, to his paradise, and to each other. God offered them all they needed to be happy, but they didn't trust him and tried to do it "their way." As Miller says, "When caught they were ashamed, but continued to struggle for control. This struggle includes the way we pass the buck and twist the truth to make us look righteous when we're caught sinning."

If, as the scripture says, "Pride goes before destruction, and a haughty spirit before a fall," then Adam and Eve were the first and fell the farthest. And the effects of this initial tendency to take God's place and be number one — inflated selfishness and pride — has spread to the farthest corners of the earth, sometimes even ending up in petty little power displays such as we saw in Marge's actions, actions that do nothing but lose friends for us.

Let's look at pride and its consequences this way. Picture someone who has climbed over everyone to get to the ladder of success and discovered it was propped up against the wrong building! And what a temptation it is for most of us to gladly direct some people we know to place their ladder on the wrong building and snicker at the results.

So how far will God let Marge — or any of us — go before we get doused with a cold bucket of reality? Fall off our ladder, so to speak. Only he knows. He evidently has a special adventure for each person in his world, an adventure that involves failure and success and lessons to be learned. Many times, because we are free to choose our own way, he lets us learn the hard way. We end up taking a long fall from our selfish little pinnacle of pride. And *then* if we're lucky, we'll remember just who we are and who God is and we can surrender to God the outcome of our lives. We need to learn — and relearn — the hard lesson that we don't have to run everything, we don't have to fix everything; we don't have to puff ourselves up with pride as we try to be the biggest frog in the puddle.

We can learn to say to God, "Please show me your will for me today" and then sit quietly back and listen. His way may be very different from the path that led us into prideful trouble, but it's always a lot better. Remember, "Not my will but thine be done," so we can live our lives in the knowledge that God is, indeed, watching with a warm and gentle pride. Amen.

www.ingramcontent.com/pod-product-compliance
Lightning Source LLC
Chambersburg PA
CBHW061654050426
42443CB00027B/3288